RUMOURS of ANGELS

RUMOURS OF ANGELS

graham kendrick

MAKE WAY MUSIC

We hope you enjoy *Rumours of Angels*. Further copies are available from your local music shop or Christian bookshop.

In case of difficulty, please contact the publisher direct by writing to:

The Sales Department
world wide worship
Buxhall
Stowmarket
Suffolk
IP14 3BW

Phone 01449 737978
Fax 01449 737834
E-mail www@kevinmayhewltd.com

Please ask for our complete catalogue of outstanding Church Music.

First published in Great Britain in 1994 by Make Way Music.

This edition © Copyright 2000 world wide worship

ISBN 1 84003 616 8
ISMN M 57004 747 5
Catalogue No: 1450193

0 1 2 3 4 5 6 7 8 9

Songbook arrangements: Chris Mitchell
Choral arrangements: Ken Burton and Steve Thompson – *You came from the highest* and *White Horse*; Ken Burton – *Earth lies spellbound*.

Cover:
Original artwork by James Kessell
Design by Jonathan Stroulger

Music setter: Donald Thomson
Proof reader: Marian Hellen

Important Copyright Information

Contents

1 Can you believe it?

Words and Music: Graham Kendrick

* Solo parts are optional

MIDDLE SECTION

Je - sus, how we love to sing your praise.

Har - mo - ni - sing with the choirs of an -

- gels as they sing! 3. Can you be - lieve

CODA

Can you be - lieve it?

3. Can you believe it?
   His name shall be called Wonderful.
   Can you believe it?
   Counsellor, Mighty God.
   Can you believe it?
   Everlasting Father.
   Can you believe it?
   He is the Prince of Peace.

4. Can you believe it?
   This is good news, good news.
   Can you believe it?
   Don't be afraid!
   Can you believe it?
   The Sun of Righteousness has dawned.
   Can you believe it?
   Joy to the world!
   Can you believe it?
   He came to seek, to save the lost.
   Can you believe it?
   Peace on earth!
   Can you believe it, (believe it),
   oh, can you believe it?

Note:
Album sequence: Intro; v.1; ch; v.2; mid; v.3;
8 bar instrumental; ch; mid; v.4; ending.

2 Rumours of angels

Words and Music: Graham Kendrick

1. Rum-ours of an-gels, vis-ions of light,
   an-gels, songs in the night,
   long-ing, eyes filled with tears,

new star ap-pear-ing, pierc-ing the night.
deep in the dan-ger, un-quench-a-ble light.
na-tions are wait-ing at the end of the years.

Town full of stran-gers sleeps in the gloom,
World full of stran-gers sleeps in the gloom,
Em-pires are fall-ing, judge-ments ap-pear,

God comes a-mong us; there is no room. 2. Rum-ours of
God comes a-mong us; there is no
God comes a-mong us; his king-dom is

3 Earth lies spellbound

Words and Music: Graham Kendrick
Choral arrangement: Ken Burton

15

come!

Christ has come, has come, our Christ has come.

Chorus

Wake up, wake up, it's Christ-mas morn-ing,

T&B

Wake up, wake up, it's Christ - mas morn - ing,

20

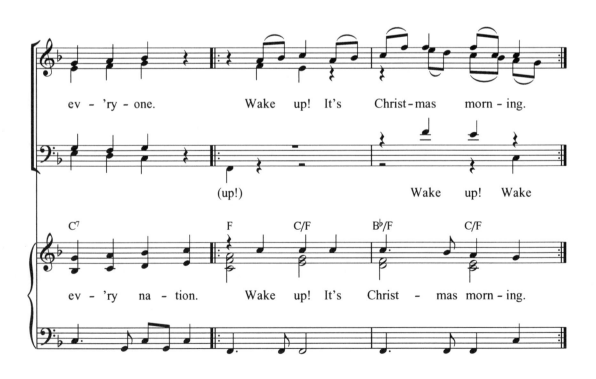

4 Nothing will ever be the same again

So many centuries

Words and Music: Graham Kendrick

1. So many centuries of watching and waiting,
but when the moment came, well nobody saw,
traders and travellers hurried by,
and life went on just like before.

2. In all the clamour just a new baby crying,
one more poor family shut out in the cold.
Nothing unusual, sad to say,
hasn't it always been this way?

3. So rare we recognise our history in the making,
meet angels unawares and pass on our way,
blind to the moment of destiny,
while precious years just slip away, slip away.

4. And now a door is standing open before you,
casting its light into the darkness around,
stop for a moment, step inside,
tonight could be your Bethlehem.

child   is   born,   a Son   is giv'n,

and his King - dom   of peace   will

ne - ver end,   ne - ver end,   no!

And

5 Thorns in the straw

Since the day the angel came

Words and Music: Graham Kendrick

1. Since the day the an-gel came it seemed that ev-'ry-thing had changed, the on-ly cer-tain thing was the child that moved with-in. On the road that would not end, wind-ing down to Beth-le-hem, so far a-way from home.

2. Just a

2. Just a blanket on the floor
   of a vacant cattle-stall,
   but there the child was born,
   she held him in her arms,
   And as she laid him down to sleep,
   she wondered - will it always be
   so bitter and so sweet.

3. Then the words of ancient seers
   tumbled down the centuries,
   . . . a virgin shall conceive . . .
   God with us . . . Prince of Peace.
   Man of Sorrows - strangest name,
   oh Joseph there it comes again,
   so bitter yet so sweet.

4. And as she watched him through the years,
   her joy was mingled with her tears,
   and she'd feel it all again,
   the glory, and the shame,
   And when the miracles began
   she wondered, who is this man,
   and where will this all end.

5. 'Til against a darkening sky,
   the son she loved was lifted high,
   and with his dying breath,
   she heard him say 'Father, forgive'.
   And to the criminal beside,
   'Today - with me in Paradise'
   so bitter yet so sweet.

6 Ain't nothing like it

Words and Music: Graham Kendrick

1. Ain't no-thing like it, this joy I'm feel-ing. Ain't no-thing like it, what can I say? Ain't no-thing like it, my head is reel-ing. Ain't no-thing like this hap-py day.

To verse

To chorus

2. Ain't no-thing - prise.

2. Ain't nothing like it,
   this wild experience;
   could not believe my
   own ears and eyes.
   I thought I'd died and
   I'd gone to heaven.
   Ain't nothing like
   this big surprise.

3. Ain't nothing like it,
   the news they told us,
   for us a Saviour,
   a baby boy;
   born in a stable,
   the One we're looking for,
   he must be heaven's pride and joy.
   (Joy, joy, joy.)

Chorus 2   *So excited,*
what a birthday party,
hallelujah O yeah!
So delighted,
we have been invited
to celebrate
his happy day.

RAP

Chorus 3   *Glory, hallelujah,*
heaven's peace and joy be to you,
everything is alright now.
Let's sing it, and shout it,
tell the world about it.
Ain't nothing like
this happy feeling.

Ain't nothing like this crazy day.
Come on and join this happy day.

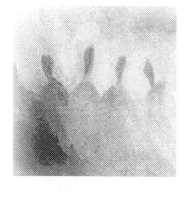

7 Seekers and dreamers

Stars in our eyes

Words and Music: Graham Kendrick

1. Stars in our eyes, we're trav-'ling moun-tains of stone and such wild hope ris-es in-side.

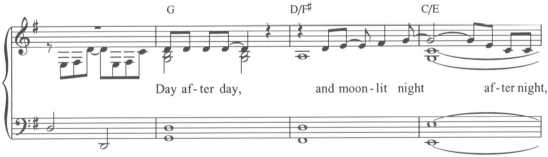

Day af-ter day, and moon-lit night af-ter night,

not know-ing where the road will end,

the road will end.

Chorus A

We are the seek - ers, the dream - ers, mys - ti - cal trav -

- 'lers, be - liev - ers, risk - ing it all on a star,

know - ing there's Some - bo - dy there. Long - ing to bring

you our trea - sures, lay at your feet the most pre - cious

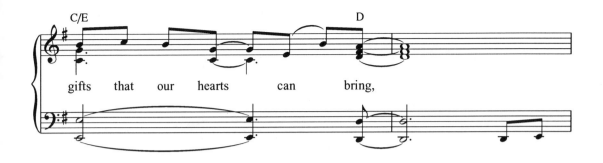

gifts   that   our   hearts   can   bring,

oh   how   we   long   to   be   there.

2. Weary and cold,
   sometimes we stumble and fall,
   and wonder why we carry on.
   But somehow this star
   has touched eternity deep
   inside our hearts, calling us near,
   leading us on.

3. When we set out,
   well we were searching for him,
   but something strange is happening;
   somehow it feels
   that he is searching for us,
   sending his star to guide us in,
   to lead us home.

Chorus B
We are the seekers, the dreamers,
mystical trav'lers, believers,
risking it all on a star,
knowing there's Someone out there.
Searching the far constellations,
seeking the source of creation;
Love is the treasure we bring,
oh how we long to be there.

8 He is here

Words and Music: Graham Kendrick

1. He is here, and we have come to wor-ship him, in his pre-sence o-pen-ing the trea-sures of our hearts. He is here, the cen-tre of our long-ings, all our rest-less jour-ney-ings are end-ed in his peace. And God is

2. He is here,
   and we have come to worship him,
   in his presence opening
   the treasures of our hearts.
   He is here,
   the One for whom the angels sing.
   Heav'n and earth are touching,
   this is a holy place.

9 What kind of greatness

Words and Music: Graham Kendrick

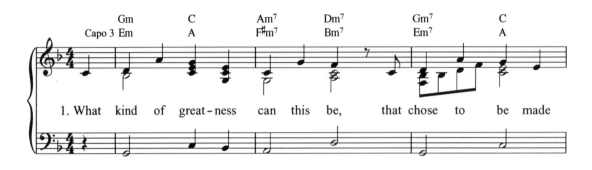

1. What kind of great-ness can this be, that chose to be made

small? Ex - chang-ing un - told ma - jes - ty, for a world so pi - ti-

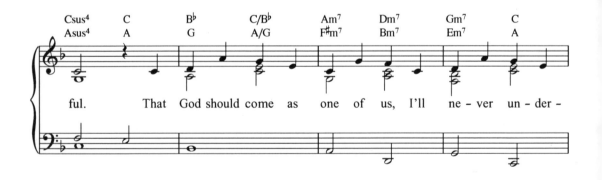

ful. That God should come as one of us, I'll ne - ver un - der-

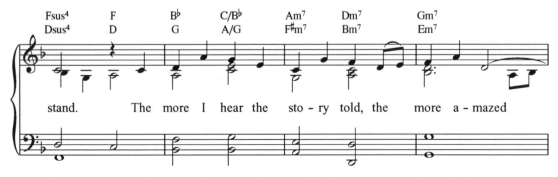

stand. The more I hear the sto - ry told, the more a - mazed

2. The One in whom we live and move,
   in swaddling cloths lies bound.
   The voice that cried, 'Let there be light',
   asleep without a sound.
   The One who strode among the stars,
   and called each one by name,
   lies helpless in a mother's arms
   and must learn to walk again.

3. What greater love could he have shown
   to shamed humanity
   yet human pride hates to believe
   in such deep humility.
   But nations now may see his grace
   and know that he is near,
   when his meek heart, his words, his works
   are incarnate in us here.

10 You came from the highest

We will sing your song

Words and Music: Graham Kendrick
Choral arrangement: Ken Burton and Steve Thompson

2. You came from the kindest,
   to suffer the cruelest,
   you are the message of love.
   You came from the purest,
   to die for the foulest,
   you are the message of love.
   Our God unrecognised,
   for ruined sinners crucified.

3. In the bustle of main street,
   the noise and the concrete,
   make us your message of love.
   In the turmoil of nations,
   or a heart's desperation,
   make us your message of love.
   Each step, each breath we take,
   yours is the love we celebrate.

Note:
1. Album sequence: ch; v1; ch; mid; v2; ch; v3; ch; ch; ch; O come . . .
2. To use on its own, omit 'O come, O come Immanuel', and end with an extra middle section.

§ *Chorus*

We will sing your song, fol-low you for e-ver. We will be your hands

We will sing your song, fol-low you for e-ver. We will be your hands

G D Am⁷ Em⁷ D D/C Am⁷

reach-ing out a-gain. Your song goes on and on, your

reach-ing out a-gain. Your song goes on and on, your

Em D G D

laugh-ter breaks the si-lence. The sea-son of your joy will

laugh-ter breaks the si-lence. The sea-son of your joy will

Am⁷ Em⁷ D D/C Am⁷

Peace to the peo-ple on earth.

Glo-ry to God in the high-est hea-ven. Peace to the peo-ple on

Peace to the peo-ple on earth.

Glo-ry to God in the high-est hea-ven. Peace to the peo-ple on

Em D/F# G D Em

To verse 2 CODA

earth.

earth.

Cmaj⁷ D D C G/B C

To verse 2 CODA

We will sing your song,

D G D

We will sing your song,

45

ne - ver, ne - ver end.

ne - ver, ne - ver end.

Em⁷   D

(may be sung as solo)
O come, O come, Im - man - u -
O

Em⁷   Em   F/E   Bm/E

el.   O come, O come, Im - man - u -
come, O come, Im - man - u - el.   O

Em   D/E   Em   F/E   Bm/E

47

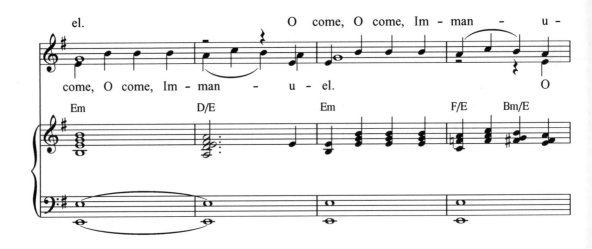

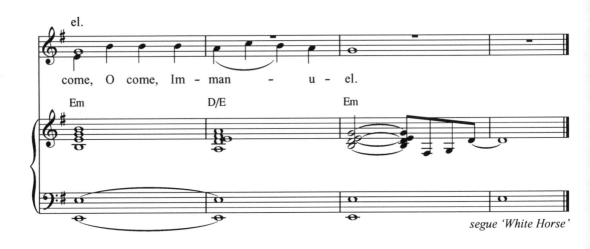

segue 'White Horse'

11 White horse

Be patient

Words and Music: Graham Kendrick
Choral arrangement: Ken Burton and Steve Thompson

Be pa-tient, be rea-dy, look up— the Lord is near.

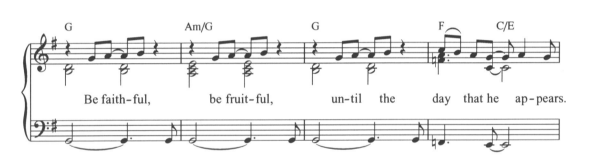

Be faith-ful, be fruit-ful, un-til the day that he ap-pears.

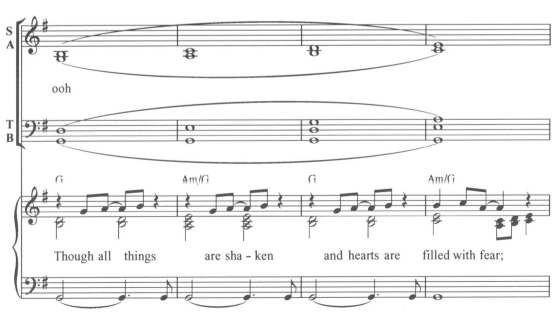

ooh

Though all things are sha-ken and hearts are filled with fear;

Come, Je - sus, come, Je - sus!' Come, deep in our

Descant

Though all things

Dsus⁴ D E♭sus⁴ E♭ A♭/C

Come!' Deep in our

hearts there's a cry, as the Spi - rit and Bride say:

Deep in our hearts a cry, Spi - rit and Bride say:

are sha - ken and hearts are filled with fear;

D♭/F A♭/E♭ B♭m⁷ D♭/E♭

hearts there's a cry, as the Spi - rit and Bride say: